THE NETWORK MARKETING BLUEPRINT TO ACHIEVING YOUR ULTIMATE FINANCIAL SUCCESS

A detailed, step-by-step guide to producing significant and immediate profits... without any of the 'fluff,' 'hype,' or 'bull.'

RON MALEZIS

Copyright © 2020 RON MALEZIS
All rights reserved. No part of this publication may be reproduced, distributed, or transmitted in any form or by any means, including photocopying, recording, or other electronic or mechanical methods, without the prior written permission of the publisher, except in the case of brief quotations embodied in critical reviews and certain other noncommercial uses permitted by copyright law.
Book Design by HMDpublishin

Here's an old, but true, proverb:
"The best time to plant a tree is 20 years ago.
The second best time is NOW."

CONTENTS

FOREWORD 7

A NEW WORLD! 9

SELF-RELIANCE: MYTH or SOLUTION? 11

CREATING YOUR PLAN 12

BEING STRATEGIC WITH YOUR CHOICES 13

REDUCING YOUR RISKS 14

LOCATION. LOCATION. LOCATION. — But Wait Just A Minute! 15

SPEED OF INCOME IS CRUCIAL 16

THERE'S ONE MORE THING 17

SO, LET'S TOTAL UP WHERE WE'RE AT 18

THERE IS ONE THING, PROVEN TIME AND TIME AGAIN 20

LET'S SEE HOW NETWORK MARKETING STACKS UP 21

IT'S NOT ALL ROSES 23

REVENUE GENERATING ACTIVITIES – BEING STRATEGIC . . 25

IMAGINE NEVER HAVING TO PROSPECT FOR PEOPLE 26

A PROVEN PLAN 27

IT GETS EVEN BETTER 28

LEVERAGING YOUR TIME FOR MAXIMUM EFFECTIVENESS	29
IT'S TIME TO TAKE ACTION	30
WHAT NOW?	31
WHY YOU NEED A BUSINESS PLAN	32
7 STEPS TO SUCCESS	34
SIMPLE VS. EASY	35
OBVIOUS ADVANTAGES	37
THERE ARE TWO KINDS OF PROSPECTS IN THE WORLD	38
WARM MARKET VS. NEW MARKET	39
WORKING YOUR NEW MARKET	41
HOW TO CONTACT YOUR LEADS	43
TAKE ACTION	45
THIS IS A PROVEN PROCESS	47
INITIAL CALL SCRIPT:	48
WRAP-UP SCRIPT:	49
HANDLING BASIC OBJECTIONS:	50
THE POWER QUESTION TECHNIQUE... AND MORE	52
VOICEMAIL MESSAGES	53
SENDING A TEXT	57
IF THEY DON'T RESPOND – SEND AN EMAIL	58
'K.I.S.S.' YOUR PROSPECTS	60
THE FORMATTED INTERVIEW PROCESS	61

GET PREPARED 63

HERE ARE YOUR INTERVIEW QUESTIONS................ 64

BEFORE WE EXPLORE HOW TO CLOSE THE SALE 70

CLOSING THE DEAL AFTER THEY'VE WATCHED A PRESENTATION 71

THE 6 QUESTION SYSTEM TO CLOSING THE DEAL 73

CLOSING WITH CONFIDENCE 77

UNDERSTANDING REJECTION...................... 79

CONDITIONS VS. OBJECTIONS 81

DO NOT FOCUS ON MAKING A SALE................... 82

ACRES OF DIAMONDS............................ 83

HOW TO ELIMINATE FAILURE 85

IN CONCLUSION 88

RESOURCES 89

Ron Malezis 91

FOREWORD

Your mission, if you decide to accept it, is to read, understand, and employ the strategies, tactics, and techniques presented here, so that you can go forth and enjoy the prosperous lifestyle of your dreams.

This is a BLUEPRINT. When followed exactly, it can deliver significant and immediate profits to you. It will also save you a great deal of time and effort and help you avoid pointless frustration.

However, let me caution you:

Just like a blueprint you might use in a construction project, this is very specific. There are details presented here to which you will need to pay very close attention. Do not gloss over the content. We've put great care into everything covered here. None of it is dispensable or unnecessary. We all get sidetracked from time to time, so you may need to review the content multiple times to keep these ideas uppermost in your mind.

Inside this blueprint you will receive a real-world overview of the current marketplace and economic conditions that you must consider. You will have the choices available to you clearly explained. There are step-by-step instructions that will give you a proven successful business plan, along with the details to act upon it. Everything from what to say, to how to say it and who to say it to is included. You'll get everything you need to do and, perhaps more importantly, what *not* to do.

FOREWORD

This is all very practical information. While there is some philosophy to give you the rationale behind how and why these techniques work, you will discover that ultimately, everything here is designed to be put into ACTION.

And there's more... a LOT more.

So now it's up to you to accept your mission and act on it.

A NEW WORLD!

We have witnessed an event that is unparalleled in our economic lives.

Our daily existence has been turned upside down by an unseen enemy. If someone had told you about these insane circumstances a year ago, wouldn't you have just laughed it off as a bad sci-fi B-movie plot?

But nobody's laughing now.

The horrifying fact is there are countless bankruptcies, shuttered businesses, and sadly even suicides, due to the financial calamity caused by the pandemic. It has affected us in ways that we could never have imagined.

Entire industries that once raked in *billions*, like travel, education, and dining, have been brought to their knees.

We have been suddenly and forcefully prevented from enjoying some of the simple pleasures we so recently took for granted.

Little things like grabbing a drink with a friend, going to a movie or concert, or even getting a haircut were either made impossible where we live or carried a heavy health and social burden.

Unemployment went from among the lowest we've ever seen in our country's history to record highs… in just a matter of weeks.

Even if you're one of the fortunate ones who still has a job to go back to, the experience of being under lock-down orders for months at a time leaves a mental and emotional scar that can't easily be erased.

And there is the nagging fear and dark uncertainty: even after the worst of this pandemic is over... WHAT IF IT HAPPENS AGAIN?

But IN EVERY CRISIS, there are those who THRIVE.

It's not that these fortunate people were somehow smarter or better prepared than others. No. They were simply POSITIONED in a such a way that no matter what was happening in the world around them, they could not only financially survive... but PROSPER.

Not at the expense of those suffering, mind you. Quite the opposite, in fact.

These industrious people have been in the position to reach out and *lend a helping hand* to those being crushed financially.

SELF-RELIANCE: MYTH or SOLUTION?

America was built on the notion of SELF-RELIANCE.

Unfortunately, some smug members of society have been fooled into thinking that this founding principle of self-reliance was either a myth or an unrealistic and outdated concept, now confined to dusty old history books.

But in reality, that powerful American spirit still lives on... and in more people than you would ever imagine.

You MUST find ways to rely on yourself, no matter what happens in the world around you. Otherwise you will suffer the harshest of consequences.

It is imperative that you find a way (or ways) to generate income which is dependent on YOU and YOUR OWN ABILITIES.

To put it bluntly, you can't count on the government, or on anyone else.

CREATING YOUR PLAN

How do you go about creating a PLAN to financially protect yourself and your family, moving forward?

Before exploring the possible solutions, you must first have the *right mindset*.

Things are changing faster than ever before.

We've got new words and strange concepts like *"social distancing"* and *"the 6 foot rule"* that have become part of our daily conversation.

YOU must change too. It's time for you to do some NEW THINKING... of the *productive kind*.

Most of what people think about during these hard times is personally *destructive* to them. That's got to stop. You've got to think in terms of *solutions* rather than the immediate problems.

The MOST OBVIOUS SOLUTION is to create an income generating activity where YOU are in control of what you earn.

Think back to the pioneer days; our country was founded and settled by people who worked for themselves.

But there are SO MANY work/job/business possibilities now. HOW in the world does one narrow down the vast number of choices to something manageable?

BEING STRATEGIC WITH YOUR CHOICES

In starting any sort of new income generating project there are multiple considerations you must weigh:

- **Your RESOURCES** — not only how much *money* you've got to work with, but also your *time* and *connections*.

- **Your current level of KNOWLEDGE.** To be direct, the less you have to learn, the shorter your learning curve will be before you start generating profits.

- **The scope of your INTERESTS.** It's hard to commit to something you're simply NOT interested in. However, your current interests CAN be broadened (In truth, you need to be more flexible than ever before).

We're going to come back to this idea of being STRATEGIC a little later. But there's another ultra-important factor you MUST CONSIDER.

REDUCING YOUR RISKS

You must analyze the RISK factors associated with any new income generating activity. In an ideal situation, you want to generate the *highest* income, as *quickly* as possible, while at the same time being exposed to the *lowest level of risk*.

For most people, THAT RULES OUT *"INVESTING"*. Many people have considered putting their money into things like the stock market, commodities, real estate, cryptocurrencies, and so on.

First, the movement of those markets is NOT something under your control, in any shape or fashion. Far from it. Outside forces control those markets.

Secondly, there exists the possibility of losing part, or ALL, of your money, as we've seen countless times over the years.

Thirdly, it takes *either* a LOT of money, or a LOT of knowledge, to be profitable as an investor... often *both*.

For the majority of people, INVESTING is little more than GAMBLING. Yes, of course there are those who win... for a time. But as recent events have shown, those gains can be wiped out very quickly.

Ultimately, you have NO CONTROL. It's all a question of getting the TIMING just right, and not getting *stuck* if, and when, the bottom drops out.

LOCATION. LOCATION. LOCATION. – But Wait Just A Minute!

It's become an adage of both the real estate and business communities. The key to success is "Location. Location. Location."

But what happens when you can't GET TO THAT LOCATION (as with the recent lockdowns)?

What happens if the MARKET CHANGES, and a location or geographic area that *once* was good *no longer is* (as we've seen with hurricanes, tornadoes, floods, wildfires… etc.)?

This is yet another RISK FACTOR we've got to include in our plan.

You need an income generating activity that can literally be done from ANYWHERE.

Of course, we want one we can do from HOME. But it's especially important that it can be done from WHEREVER you are — no matter the city, state, or country.

These days, that location risk factor can be *completely eliminated* with a steady INTERNET CONNECTION.

SPEED OF INCOME IS CRUCIAL

Many people have been unfairly prejudiced against the idea of "get-rich-quick schemes". The term itself is a pejorative. It's become associated with things that are illegal or immoral. And that's a shame, because it's NOT ALWAYS TRUE!

Of COURSE, you want to do something that is moral, ethical, and beneficial to others. But the SPEED at which one earns money is also *very* important.

Let me illustrate. If you earned a MILLION DOLLARS but it took you 50 YEARS to do it, that would be only $20,000 a year. Not such a big deal, right?

However, if you earned that same MILLION DOLLARS in only 5 YEARS, (10 X faster) that would be far more impressive, yes? *Of course*!

It's not the amount, it's the speed at which it happened.

So, whatever you do, you must look for things that have the potential to GENERATE PROFIT QUICKLY... again, with AS LOW OF A RISK AS POSSIBLE.

THERE'S ONE MORE THING

If you are going to take the time to pursue a valid income generating activity, then there's one more, very important consideration:

THE DEMAND for your product or service.

If nobody's LOOKING for what you've got, then little else matters.

But demand can change — like fads, fashion, or technology — so you want something that has been PROVEN to stand the test of time.

SO, LET'S TOTAL UP WHERE WE'RE AT

Here's a list of the things we've discussed so far that YOU NEED in order to SUCCESSFULLY PROTECT YOURSELF & YOUR FAMILY FINANCIALLY:

☑ You need an income generating activity that has LOW RISK.

- That means it doesn't cost much to get started.
- There are no debts you'll need to incur (like mortgages or business loans).
- There's a low overhead to keep it going.

☑ **You *must* be able to do it ANYWHERE.**

- You are not confined to doing business in a particular location.
- You can carry out your tasks by computer, tablet/iPad, or with a mobile phone.
- You only need internet access.

☑ **It needs to be something that can GENERATE PROFITS QUICKLY.**

☑ **It needs to be something where YOU HAVE A HIGH LEVEL**

OF CONTROL.

- ☑ It has to be **SIMPLE** enough that you can **LEARN IT QUICKLY.**

- ☑ It must be moral, ethical, and **BENEFICIAL** to others.

- ☑ There should exist a constant, never-ending **DEMAND** for what you've got.

Whew! That's quite a wishlist.

Is there ANYTHING that can fit this extensive list of demands?

THERE IS ONE THING, *PROVEN* TIME AND TIME AGAIN

Obviously, there are exceedingly few businesses that can fit EVERY SINGLE CRITERION on that list. Here is the best one:

Network Marketing, also known as MLM, has been PROVEN over the past SEVEN (7) DECADES to meet every single objective on our list above.

In fact, it is considered to be the *ultimate shortcut* for financially protecting you and your family, and for achieving personal wealth!

LET'S SEE HOW NETWORK MARKETING STACKS UP

Here's how Network Marketing compares to our extensive list of requirements.

It doesn't require significant cash or a costly overhead to get started, and you certainly don't need to incur massive amounts of debt. In most cases, you can begin with a few hundred dollars — often even less.

The overhead to run a Network Marketing business is EXTREMELY LOW.

Other than what you purchase for yourself each month, there is no inventory to buy. You don't have to maintain, track, store, or ship anything, as the parent companies do all that for you.

Compared to traditional businesses, you don't need fancy facilities or a bunch of employees. You don't need advanced degrees or any formal schooling. You don't even need a particular employment background work experience to get started.

It's a SIMPLE business, and one that is EASY to learn.

These days, with many MLM companies, you truly have a *worldwide marketplace*. Quite a number of them operate successfully in North, Central, and South America, Asia, and Europe.

This allows for the GREATEST POSSIBLE CONSUMER DEMAND. (That is a HUGE point to consider.)

Contrary to what you may have thought previously, the main thing any Network Marketing company offers is the OPPORTUNITY TO MAKE MONEY FROM HOME... regardless of the product or service any particular company provides.

As anyone can plainly see, *NOW*, MORE THAN AT ANY TIME IN RECORDED HISTORY, there is an increasing number of people who are actively seeking legitimate ways to make money from home.

Network Marketing companies are in the PEOPLE DEVELOPMENT business. Their training focuses on helping people improve important human qualities. You will see average people grow in their abilities to communicate, lead others, and maintain a more positive outlook. Those are all very beneficial qualities and are some of the unseen advantages of having a business like this.

IT'S NOT ALL ROSES

Let's be real here, and not oversimplify things. While it's true there are MANY benefits of starting a home business with a Network Marketing company, it's not all roses.

Just like in traditional business, there is a significant failure rate.

Unfortunately, there are far too many people who approach this profession as if it's *"The Lazy Man's Way to Riches"*.

Let's get clear on a couple of things here. This is NOT a get-rich-quick 'scheme'. It is a BUSINESS with rules that must be followed and procedures that must be learned and applied.

In order to be successful, one must gain some new skills and take the time to properly develop them.

THE BIGGEST ADVANTAGE

The biggest advantage Network Marketing provides can be summed up in one word: <u>LEVERAGE</u>.

Leverage allows you to MULTIPLY your results, and it AMPLIFIES your power *without consuming any additional resources or energy.*

Compared to other types of business, being successful in Network Marketing is NOT based how much work you can do personally.

Instead, this is all about leveraging the TIME and EFFORTS of the team you build.

In a traditional business, if you are working at it for 20 hours a week, you'll be paid on the results you generate with those 20 hours.

Here's how LEVERAGE works to your advantage with Network Marketing.

Let's say you build a team of just 16 people who each work 20 hours. That's a total of 16 people X 20 hours or 320 hours in total. You can be PAID on the results created from 320 hours instead of merely the 20 that you put in personally.

Let's take it just one step further and say you have a team of just 50 members putting in 20 hours a week. Now you can be paid on the efforts and results of 1,000 hours a week.

Eventually, some people become so successful that after just a few years, they have very large teams built. Those people continue to put forth their efforts to grow their business. When your team gets big enough, your income is effectively on AUTOPILOT.

That means that no matter WHAT happens to you personally, your income will continue month after month. It is the very definition of RESIDUAL INCOME.

You do the work ONCE, and get paid over, and over, and over again.

REVENUE GENERATING ACTIVITIES – BEING STRATEGIC

Here's how to speed up your financial results, along with increasing the results of every person on your team:

You must engage in activities that *produce revenue*. Do not waste time with activities that merely keep you busy but don't create income.

The most important revenue generating activity in this type of business is the introduction of new reps.

At this moment, **MORE PEOPLE THAN EVER BEFORE** are actively looking for legitimate ways to make money from home.

Can you imagine how profitable it would be if you had a CONSTANT SUPPLY of those interested prospects delivered to you on a weekly basis?

IMAGINE *NEVER* HAVING TO PROSPECT FOR PEOPLE

As just discussed, you must avoid time wasting activities and focus on revenue generating ones.

Imagine for a moment what it would be like if you had a CONSTANT SUPPLY of people who had already stepped-up and identified themselves as being interested in starting a home business.

Wouldn't it be great if you could get the contact info of the millions upon millions of people who are, *right now*, looking for ways to make extra money working from home?

STOP IMAGINING… that's exactly what you're about to discover.

A PROVEN PLAN

A proven business plan is to work *pre-qualified leads.*

By that, I mean people who have responded to online advertising, "raised their hands" requesting more information, and answered several questions to qualify their level of interest.

Your time can then be spent directly reaching out to people who have *identified themselves* as wanting to make additional money with a home-based business.

Suppose your plan is to work 20 hours a week and, during that time, contact between 150 and 300 people.

First of all, it would be difficult to find that many people to contact each week if you didn't have a proven system in place.

Working pre-qualified leads is the very best way to maximize the effectiveness of your own time. It's employing TIME LEVERAGE to your personal advantage.

Now picture this. Suppose you had a team of 50 people, each of them like you. They all wanted to work 20 hours a week and planned to contact between 150 to 300 pre-qualified prospects a week.

To keep our arithmetic easy, let's say those 50 reps were able to contact 200 people a week.

That's a total of 10,000 prospects a week being contacted by your group. They're reaching out, making presentations, and inviting them to look at your business opportunity. With numbers like that, you could generate some pretty impressive incomes.

IT GETS EVEN BETTER

When a person joins your business through a highly organized system like the one we just described, it will feel comfortable and natural for them to use the same approach. After all, they know for certain the plan works, since it's how they got enrolled.

A systematic approach like this will enable your team to grow quite large, and do it much faster than those typical reps who work their businesses in a haphazard fashion.

Understanding the amazing power of leverage means you don't need a big group of people in order to earn a lot of money. You just need a dedicated group of people who are productive because they are working a clear and proven system.

Think about it. A team of just 100 reps reaching out to 200 prospects a week equals 20,000 contacts. An impressive number by any standard.

LEVERAGING YOUR TIME FOR MAXIMUM EFFECTIVENESS

Look. You can spend your time building funnels, writing sales copy, and testing ads while also doing a ton of prospecting and searching for qualified people.

OR you can spend your time making presentations and closing business with leads who came to you pre-qualified.

Remember, it's about time leverage. Stay focused on money making activities that are duplicatable.

Don't quit. Be consistent. And always know that the law of large numbers will NEVER fail you.

IT'S TIME TO TAKE ACTION

It is up to YOU to come up with workable plan to FINANCIALLY PROTECT YOURSELF & YOUR FAMILY.

We've listed a good number of critical considerations to factor into that plan.

You've gained an understanding of the important things you DO want, and received fair warning about the things you DON'T.

You realize just how vital it is to be in control of your own financial future and the necessity of having a new income generating project of your own.

The one proven business that fits ALL the criteria we've laid out is Network Marketing. It's a simple business, but never mistake it for an *easy* business. There are skills you must learn that are crucial to your success.

Bear in mind that the greatest advantage here is LEVERAGE.

Leverage is the most important power that will enable you to achieve financial freedom. You must understand it and use it to your advantage.

Do that, and you and your family will have the financial protection you seek, and more... for you will be well on your way to creating lasting and sustainable wealth!

WHAT NOW?

Be sure to review this report as many times as you need. People often find they pick up new ideas from re-reading reports like this after a day or two.

Nothing happens without taking action.

If you don't know which Network Marketing companies to investigate, fill out our survey form and we'll have a few hand-selected advisors from top-rated companies contact you for a private conversation.

Click here to FILL OUT A SURVEY and SPEAK WITH AN ADVISOR.

If you've already selected a company, <u>*congratulations!*</u>

Now it's time to employ a smart business plan.

WHY YOU NEED A BUSINESS PLAN

In the next section, you're going to get "7 Steps to Success" that will enable you to get off to the FASTEST START possible. These are practical, not merely philosophical. Each one of these 7 Steps is an *actionable* item.

But first, here is a FACT.

Network Marketing has been PROVEN, time and time again, to be the *ultimate* FINANCIAL SHORTCUT for achieving personal wealth.

However, many people fail at it because they simply do not treat their business with the serious respect it deserves.

This is NOT a get-rich-quick 'scheme'. It is a BUSINESS with rules that must be followed and procedures that must be learned and applied.

That is why you need to have a business plan, *and stick to it*.

The more clear and straightforward your plan is, the easier it will be to achieve the success you desire. The opposite is also true. If your plan is complex and difficult, you'll have a harder time following it and could face frustration, even defeat.

It has been my thoughtful observation that far too many people unnecessarily complicate what is essentially a very simple business. That is why I've distilled the process down to just 7 easily digestible steps.

The more you deviate from the time-tested and proven 7 steps covered in the next section, the less success you will have. But the more you *focus* on them, the faster and more lasting your success will be.

You've heard of the K.I.S.S. principle? It stands for **K**eep **I**t **S**imple, **S**weetheart (or, **K**eep **I**t **S**hort & **S**weet). That's why these 7 Steps to Success are so effective. They are short, simple, and easily understood. Even more importantly, you can immediately see yourself being able to put them into action.

7 STEPS TO SUCCESS

To achieve success with your home business, you only need to do these 7 simple things.

1. Talk to people (the more, the better).
2. Invite some of them to look at your presentation materials.
3. Follow up to see who has looked and who hasn't.
4. Sort the ones who are interested from the ones who are not.
5. Enroll the ones who are interested in your products and/or your business.
6. Help new members get started by using your products the right way.
7. Help members who also want to generate income to learn and apply these 7 steps.

Then, we REPEAT those steps over, and over, and over again.

Those are your **7 STEPS TO SUCCESS.**

Stay faithful to those steps. Whenever you catch yourself deviating from them, bring yourself back. Stay on course. Don't waste time on distractions. Focus your time on those revenue generating activities. Ignore everything else.

The bottom line is the more closely you can adhere to these steps, the faster you will achieve your goals and begin to enjoy the lifestyle of your dreams.

SIMPLE VS. EASY

One thing you can count on is that we will always tell it to you straight. That's why I've got both a warning for you... and some very GOOD NEWS.

First, the warning. **Don't be fooled!**

Just because something is supposed to be SIMPLE, doesn't mean there's no effort or skill involved. People often make the mistake of thinking that things described as being SIMPLE are the same as being EASY.

NOPE! In fact, there's a HUGE difference between the two.

Winning a basketball game is SIMPLE.
Put the ball through the hoop more times than your opponent.
But it's not EASY.

Losing weight is SIMPLE.
Burn more calories than you consume.
But it's not EASY.

Becoming financially free is SIMPLE.
Earn more money than you spend.
But it's not EASY.

Being successful with your home business is the same way. It is all based on performing very SIMPLE tasks like these:

- Make personal contact with new people every day.

- Invite receptive people to look at your business presentation.
- Enroll the people who like your business presentation.
- Teach others how to do the previous steps.

As you can plainly see, those are all very SIMPLE tasks to understand. But, they may not necessarily be EASY for you to do.

However, like I said earlier, **I have GOOD NEWS for you.**

Building your home business can be made MUCH EASIER when you employ a STRATEGIC PLAN and stick to it.

Suppose:

- you <u>never</u> had to *search* for people who wanted to start a home business (NO prospecting!)
- you had pre-qualified prospects delivered directly to you to daily
- all you had to do was connect with them and invite the interested ones to take a look at your presentation

That would make life a LOT EASIER wouldn't it?

Keep in mind that you'd still have to work on yourself and improve your communication and selling skills. You'll need to develop some *finesse*.

Even BETTER NEWS is that we here at Lead Power not only provide you with as many pre-qualified prospects as you can handle, we will also TEACH YOU the best ways to contact them. And we'll even train you for FREE!

But before we do that, let's look at the significant and obvious advantages you have available to you.

OBVIOUS ADVANTAGES

Network Marketing has a long list of favorable benefits that provide you obvious advantages over traditional business and nearly every other way to make one's fortune.

Here are a few that immediately come to mind:

- NO large cash investments
- NO need to take out loans or mortgages
- NO costly overhead
- NO inventory to maintain, track, store, or ship
- NO fancy facilities or employees

And the list goes on. But as important as those things are, the greatest advantage Network Marketing gives you can be summed up in one single word: **LEVERAGE.**

Leverage allows you to MULTIPLY your results, and it AMPLIFIES your power *without consuming any more resources or energy.*

You see, being successful in Network Marketing is NOT based how much work YOU can do. Instead it is all about leveraging the time and efforts of your TEAM.

THERE ARE TWO KINDS OF PROSPECTS IN THE WORLD

When you come right down to it, there are only TWO (2) kinds of prospects in the world who might be interested in your products or your business opportunity: the people you know and the people you don't.

OK. Don't laugh. I know it sounds silly, but that's the best way to go about building your team.

Since the beginning of our profession, back in the 1950's, everyone who has ever joined a Network Marketing company has been told to make a list of the people they know, and then to start contacting them.

It has been proven to work for decades. This is how the vast majority of people who have become wealthy through our profession have done it.

The term used to describe the people on the list of the people you know is your "WARM MARKET".

WARM MARKET VS. NEW MARKET

Here's a viewpoint some may consider controversial.

While everyone in Network Marketing has been told list and contact their warm market contacts, it is my position that they've been taught THE WRONG WAY to do it.

Now, don't get your feelings hurt, because I'm going to show you exactly how to FIX IT.

First, for the purposes of an ultra-clear definition, your "warm market" consists of the people *you know* plus the people you *meet* at events, through friends — heck, even at a coffee shop.

Now, of course, not everybody in your warm market is interested in making money working from home. In fact, as a rule of thumb, it's somewhere between 10-15%.

One of the most common pitfalls of working your warm market is that you can spend a lot of time on the phone catching up on everything you haven't talked about since the last time you spoke.

Let's be real. You simply can't spend an hour on the phone chatting with one of your old friends from years ago and actually be productive.

Besides that, it's awkward to call someone you haven't spoken to for a long time, only to then have to switch to your *real agenda*.

This is why you must GET OUT OF *YOUR* LIST, and into *THEIR* LIST as quickly as possible.

Let me restate this. You must STOP calling people you know as early in the process as possible, and switch to speaking with the people your NEW RECRUIT knows.

Once again... **get out of YOUR list, and into THEIR list.**

This is why you must use the concept of 3 WAY CALLS to be effective.

A 3 WAY CALL is where your new recruit introduces you over the phone to someone in their warm market. There are 3 of you on the phone at the same time, hence the name.

It is far more persuasive for your guest to speak with an authoritative stranger than to speak with the friend they've known for years.

(By the way, you'll learn a lot about the best ways to do 3 Way Calls in our FREE company training videos.)

And here's something else to keep in mind: most people's warm market is usually around 100 to 300 people.

By contrast, there are over **2 MILLION people *every month*** looking for new ways to make extra money working from home. These are "new market" prospects — new to you, because you don't know them yet. There's A LOT of them, and they have shown they are already INTERESTED in making money from home.

Which do *you* think is the better market to tap?

Keep in mind, you can always go back to contacting your warm market. But once you have a system of calling and closing leads, you will have built up your skills, become more articulate, and will have real-world RESULTS under your belt. And that will make you far more effective and persuasive with your warm market.

That makes perfect sense, now doesn't it?

WORKING YOUR NEW MARKET

A proven successful, *leveraged* business plan is to WORK PRE-QUALIFIED LEADS.

Doing this enables you to leverage your TIME by directly reaching out to LEADS who have already identified themselves as wanting to make additional money in a home-based business.

Think of it.

No time wasted searching for interested parties. NO PROSPECTING!

Instead, you'd be focused on sorting through people who have said they are actively looking, and MAKING PRESENTATIONS to them.

Let's throw some gas on the fire. As you know, the idea here is to engage in activities that are duplicatable by anyone you recruit to your team.

Instead of doing it alone, imagine having a small team of 50 people working 20 hours a week, with each of them contacting 100 LEADS a week.

That's **5,000 prospects a week / more than 20,000 prospects a month** that your group would be reaching out to, making presentations, and inviting them to look at your business opportunity.

Just IMAGINE the kinds of results that could create!

WORKING YOUR NEW MARKET

Working your new market, pre-qualified leads, is clearly the greatest and most OBVIOUS ADVANTAGE you could ask for when building your business.

Make your life easier.

Place an order for leads. We'll even start you off with 10 FREE LEADS to demonstrate our sincerity and increase your confidence in our system. Get your 10 **FREE LEADS** here.

Before you begin calling them, it's best to have a clear plan and know in advance what to say to them.

Now, let's talk about the best ways to contact your leads.

HOW TO CONTACT YOUR LEADS

The scripts and wording you'll see in the following sections have been proven to work for many years. These powerful techniques were extremely effective for people like *you*, people who took action.

The ideas and approaches you'll learn here are designed to be used as a guideline; you can *personalize* the specific details to suit your particular business.

Using scripts is *the most effective way* to gain consistency and to learn the language skills necessary to be effective when talking to prospects on the phone. Working with proven scripts is also a great thing to teach the people on your team. This way, you are training them to use the same presentation method. This helps you build a solid base faster.

Always remember, this is a *SORTING* business...

(not one where you need to do a lot of convincing.)

Do NOT waste time with uncooperative or disinterested prospects.

Instead, search for and focus on those prospects who are *open to learning*, and who genuinely seek an opportunity to earn money from home.

TAKE ACTION

Being successful with your networking business is more about sorting than selling. These scripts will help you sort and qualify prospects so that you can present your business opportunity to the right people.

Personally, I have enjoyed more than 25 years of experience in Network Marketing and have built teams of over 100,000 distributors. I speak with the authority gained through my own experiences. The effective use of scripts is very powerful when qualifying your prospects. It gives you a clear track to run on without having to worry about what you're going to say next.

Remember, Network Marketing is a simple business which requires activities that others are able to duplicate.

In the next section, I have provided you with the initial calling script and how to handle some of the most basic objections.

I've also included scripts for texting and for voicemail messages. These are for when you can't reach a prospect immediately. It is important to leave a compelling message that will help you create interest rather than 'winging it' and risk turning off a prospect.

In addition, I have included an effective email follow-up for people you haven't been able to reach over the phone.

You will also discover some powerfully effective techniques for closing the deal. You'll get the right things to say — wording that has proven successful over time — together with the psychology

TAKE ACTION

behind how it works.

These time-tested and proven scripts will help get you going and boost your confidence so that you get the results you're looking for and become profitable.

THIS IS A PROVEN PROCESS

This is *not* an experiment. This is *not* a bunch of theory or mere philosophy. What you get in this blueprint is a field-tested process that has been proven to work for many years.

Say the right thing to the right people and you'll get the right results.

Say the wrong things and watch out, because *anything* can happen.

This is why true professionals know what they are going to say in advance.

Something IMPORTANT to consider when working with scripts:

Most of the time, when you ask a question, WAIT for them to answer.

However, sometimes in these scripts there will be times you'll ask a question where you don't want a reply. You are actually just making a point, and no answer is required.

You'll see a blank line _____ in the script indicating where it is their turn to respond.

INITIAL CALL SCRIPT:

> Hi (their first name),
>
> My name is (your first name). I'm calling you because you recently expressed an interest in making some additional income working from home!
>
> (Do not stop and wait for a response. Go directly to question 1.)
>
> 1. Are you more interested in a part-time or full-time option? _____
>
> 2. Would you be interested in just a job or in becoming an independent business owner, where you can set your own hours and income? _____
>
> 3. Provided you qualify, how much time would you be willing to invest in a business venture on a weekly basis? _____
>
> 4. Based on finding the right business, how much income would it take to get you committed to working (X) hours? _____

WRAP-UP SCRIPT:

> *I think I have something that could fit what you're looking for!*
>
> *I need 10 Minutes of your time to watch a video. It will explain everything we do! This should give you a really good idea of what's involved, and it will let us go further in your search... Would now be a good time to watch it? _____*
>
> *[If YES]: Great. Here's the link.*
>
> *[If NO]: That's OK. How soon can you watch it? _____*

HANDLING BASIC OBJECTIONS:

Before getting into the scripted wording, always remember that your goal is to create VALUE. When you are able to successfully create a greater value in what you are offering than the cost of getting started, people will eagerly join you.

1) Don't have any money!

A) I can appreciate that. Tell me, how many years have you been in the workforce...15...20?_____ So, you mean to tell me you have been in the workforce for (X) years and you don't have ($500-$1,000) to invest in a business that could create true wealth in the next 3-6 months? How Does that FEEL? _____

B) Isn't that the EXACT reason you should be looking at doing something about it? Something unique, out-of-the-box — something YOU own? _____

C) Let me ask you this. If your hot water heater (or refrigerator, furnace, tires on car vandalized, etc.) were to give out and you needed $600 to replace it immediately, how long would it take you to FIND the money? _____

2) I don't have the time!

A) What's your short-term plan to overcome that situation? _____ And Your long-term plan? _____

B) If I could show you how you could begin leveraging your time with the efforts of a marketing team that I will assist you in building, would it be worth your time to take a serious look? _____

C) If you continue doing what you are doing, how long will it take for you to get your time back? _____

D) Do you like having no time? Do you enjoy what you are doing that leaves you with no time? _____ If I could show you an exit strategy to that situation, would take a serious look? _____

E) Do you feel like your life is not your own? When will you be ready to take your life back? I can show you a way. _____

3) I'm looking for a job!

How long have you been looking for a job? _____Hmmmm. I see. *(Go directly to the question or questions below that best fit the situation.)*

A) Would you be open to making extra money by building an independent business that doesn't prevent you from looking for a job? _____

B) Have you ever considered operating your own business where you can create the kind of income you would expect from a job, but have no ceiling on the level of income you can create? _____

C) Have you ever considered taking the skills and talents that you bring to the marketplace and utilizing them to create an income stream through your own business? _____

D) Have you ever considered having the freedom to create as much income as you want based on your effort in operating your own business (from home) rather than being confined to an income cap at a regular job? _____

E) Have you ever considered what it might be like if your commute was down the carpeted freeway from your bedroom to your home office, instead of the asphalt freeway to someone else's business that you work for 15, 30, or even 60 minutes away? _____

THE POWER QUESTION TECHNIQUE... AND MORE

These are some very important points to keep in mind.

Here's a power question technique. It is often far better to ask an **"Either/Or"** question than a **"Yes/No"** question.

For example, don't ask *"Are you looking for a part time income?"* INSTEAD USE YOUR POWER QUESTION TECHNIQUE: **"Are you looking for a part-time OR a full-time income?"**

Also, when you get your prospect on the phone, **NEVER ASK if they signed up online.** ASSUME they did, otherwise we wouldn't have their information.

Next... when handling basic objections, sometimes giving a SIMPLE ANSWER can solve someone's mental indecision far easier than anything else. It is often better for you to answer their questions with a simple *"Yes", "No"* or *"Maybe"* than it is for you to give an elaborate long-winded answer.

Learn the responses to these objections. Commit them to memory. Make them a natural part of your conversation, and you can use them whenever appropriate.

VOICEMAIL MESSAGES

The *majority* of people won't answer the phone when you call. That's because either they don't recognize your number, or they are busy doing something else.

At this point, you need to leave a voicemail (VM) message.

Whether or not your prospect responds depends on the quality of the message you leave.

You can't just use the right words, you must sound like someone they want to speak with.

Your voicemail message needs to be simple and to the point.

Leaving a good voicemail message is IMPORTANT!

People have call screening on their phones. If they don't recognize your phone number, they may let it go to voicemail. So, it's important that you have a brief, concise message with a clear call to action.

Your message needs to be short, clear, and to the point. It is NOT an opportunity meeting.

VOICEMAIL MESSAGES

> (1st Message)
>
> *Hi (their first name). This is (your first name) calling from (your city, state).*
>
> *You expressed interest in learning more about our home-based income project.*
>
> *I just wanted to follow up, help you get all the information you need and answer any questions. Could you please return my call? (leave your phone number here).*
>
> *I really think you'll like what we have, and I'm looking forward to speaking with you for a few minutes.*
>
> *By the way, if I happen to be busy on another call, please leave your phone number and the best time for me to call you back. Once again, this is (your first name) and my phone number is (leave your number slowly and clearly). Have a great day!*

2nd and FINAL MESSAGE

Fear of loss is a powerful motivator.

A final call voicemail drop is a great last-chance call to action. Leave this brief, concise message with a firm but FRIENDLY tone of voice.

This will OFTEN get people to call you back. Many times, they will even apologize for not calling you back sooner.

(2nd Message)

Hi (their first name). This is (your first name) calling again from (your city, state).

I'm leaving you a second and FINAL message as a reminder.

You had requested information about our home-based income project.

I wanted to try you one last time so that I can get you all the information you need and answer any questions you may have.

If you're still interested in a home-based income, please return my call. My number is (leave your phone number).

I really think you'll like what you see and I'm looking forward to speaking with you.

Once again, my phone number is (leave your number clearly). I hope we speak soon.

VOICEMAIL MESSAGES

REMEMBER...

If you want people to call you back, they must first *understand* you. Speak clearly. Don't rush. Be articulate with your words. If you have a thick accent, do what you can to reduce it. Sound friendly, but don't go overboard. Don't be overly familiar. Do not call them 'buddy', 'bud', 'pal', 'brother', 'dear', 'honey', 'darling', or any other terms you might use if you were speaking with a personal friend.

SENDING A TEXT

Since it is becoming more and more common for people to ignore their voicemails, you should TEXT them.

One of the biggest advantages of texting is they are read nearly 100% of the time, so you can be confident your message will be seen.

The most important thing to do is CREATE CURIOSITY. You want to give people a reason to call you back. You do NOT want to deliver any sort of presentation.

That means, keep it brief. Mention that you are contacting them in regard to earning additional income working from home and that you want to set up a time to discuss their options.

Some Reps prefer to send a text even before calling. This is purely a matter of *personal preference*. Either calling first or texting first can work very well. Just be sure to follow the additional scripts, as mentioned above, once you make contact.

EXAMPLE:

"Hi (their first name). (Your first name) here. You requested info about making money from home. I am following up as promised and have important information to give you. Please give me a call to set up a time to discuss your options."

IF THEY DON'T RESPOND – SEND AN EMAIL

The sad fact is that there will still be some people who won't respond even after you leave a VM and send a TEXT. However, that doesn't mean they're not interested.

It could be they just have other things going on that you're not aware of.

Occasionally, you may even get a phone number that doesn't work. It usually means that the person doesn't want to be contacted by phone.

In either case, the next step is to send a simple email (key word: 'simple').

Do NOT send them a bunch of information about you, your company, or your product, in the hopes they'll be interested.

Instead, just let them know you left a VM and sent a TEXT. Ask for them to get back to you so you can set up a time to discuss their options.

EXAMPLE:

Hi, (their first name).

This is (your first name) from (your city, state).

I just wanted you to know that I've been trying to follow up as promised, but unfortunately, I haven't been able to reach you by phone.

The reason I called is that you recently requested information from us about an exciting and profitable home-based income project. I wanted to make sure you got any information or answers you might need.

I don't know whether or not you'd be a good fit for our project yet. But I'd really like the opportunity to understand what you're looking for and learn a bit more about you.

Could you do me a small favor, please? Would you mind responding to this email (or give me a return call) and let me know if you're still looking for some extra income?

I'd really appreciate it.

If you already found something else or are no longer interested, no worries. Just drop me a quick email and let me know, so I can take you off my list. OK?

Thanks again (their first name), I hope we get to meet and talk soon.

Thanks in advance,
(Your first and last name)
(Put your phone number and email address here)

'K.I.S.S.' YOUR PROSPECTS

K.I.S.S. = Keep It Short & Sweet.

Do NOT get long-winded during any of your first contacts, whether it's by phone, text, or email.

Get to the point. Do it politely. Keep your eye on the goal.

Your goal is getting to the next step, which is AN INTERVIEW with your prospect.

THE FORMATTED INTERVIEW PROCESS

Once you have your prospect on the phone, you want to engage them in an actual conversation.

Before you launch into delivering any information about what you have to offer, you need to collect information about the person you're speaking with. You want to know enough about them to determine whether or not this is someone who would be a good new recruit. You need to qualify them.

Think of It like a JOB INTERVIEW.

YOU are the one with the opportunity your prospect has "applied for". They are the candidates. YOU are "The Boss". The candidate must be QUALIFIED for the position.

Please, you should NEVER FORGET THAT.

When one goes on an actual job interview, the person doing the hiring asks a lot of questions before ever telling the candidate about the company, the products, the job description, or the pay. It should be the same way here.

You are going to conduct a FORMATTED INTERVIEW with your new candidate.

To make the process easier, here are some of the very best ques-

THE FORMATTED INTERVIEW PROCESS

tions to ask, in order to properly qualify your leads.

These questions will enable you to establish productive conversations quickly, and efficiently sort out the 'sour apples'. That way, you can properly focus on your best prospects: the 'ripe apples'.

Be cautious! Some of these questioning techniques are very powerful. Using them properly will cause you get to know your prospects extremely well. You don't have time to do this with everyone. You want to quickly eliminate those who are not good prospects, even if you enjoy talking to them, because they will use up your time and not join your business.

GET PREPARED

Before speaking with any prospects, take the time to thoroughly review the entire questioning process. Do not skimp on this step. You need to get comfortable with ALL these questions in advance. This way you'll be able to jump to the questions that are most appropriate to keep the conversation going. Practice by reading them out loud. Become familiar with each section of questions. As your prospect responds, you will be able to judge which questions to ask next in order to encourage the flow of information.

In the following section, you will see main questions that will give you the big picture. Many of those 'big picture' questions have follow-ups that will help you sharpen your focus and give you greater clarity of what your prospect is thinking and feeling.

Then, at the end, once you have collected enough information, you will see specific closing techniques to use in bringing your new prospects on board.

Be sure to keep these important points in mind. You will NOT ask every question on this list. Pick and choose the ones that will lead you to your goal.

When you ask a question, <u>wait for an answer</u>. Listen to what they say. Do not talk over them. Take notes on their answers, so you can refer back to them later.

Keep these questions handy during each interview, and you will never be at a loss for words.

HERE ARE YOUR INTERVIEW QUESTIONS

Why are you interested in a home business at this time?

_____

How long have you been considering a home business?

_____

Have you looked at any yet, or do you have one in mind already?

- **[If YES]: When?**
- What kind of business?
- What appeals to you about it?
- What don't you like about it?
- **[If NO]: Why not?**
- Do you have an idea of what you're looking for?
- Are you open to the best suggestions?

_____

WHICH of these would you say is your HIGHEST PRIORITY when deciding what kind of business to have: *Income potential? Speed of income? Residual income? Flexible schedule? Ease of learn-*

ing? Type of product or service? Who you're working with?

- Why?
- What would be next most important?
- What is least important to you on that list?

_____

How familiar are you with the idea of "residual income"?

- What does that mean to you?
- Have you ever had residual income before?
- How important is that to you?

_____

What kind of work do you do now?

- How long have you been doing it?
- Why do you do that kind of work?
- How secure is your job at this time?

_____

How long have you been out of work?

- How are you getting by now?
- How long can you last like that?

_____

Are you looking for a job now?

- Looking for work in the same field or something different?
- How's it going?

HERE ARE YOUR INTERVIEW QUESTIONS

- What are your prospects?
- Are you close to being hired?
- How's that make you feel?

_____

What sort of schedule do you work now?

- Are you willing to devote a few hours a week to your home business?
- How many hours a week would you be willing to work from home?
- What sort of schedule do you think is best for you?
- Could you commit to that?

_____

About how much do you earn a month/year with your present job?

- How long did it take you to get up to that amount?
- How much were you earning when you started?

_____

Are you looking for something to supplement your current income, or to replace it?

- How much would you need to be earning by the end of 90 days to make you feel that your new business is worth it?
- How much would you hope to earn in your first year?

_____

How much additional money are you looking to earn each month?

- How'd you come up with that number?
- What are you hoping to accomplish with that money?
- OR/ What do you plan to do with that money?
- How soon do you need it?

_____

Tell me a little about your family situation now.

- Married/divorced/single?
- Children/how many/ages?
- Any kids preparing for college?
- Got money set aside for college?
- How much do you expect that to cost you?

_____

What do you like to do for fun?

- Got any hobbies?
- What does something like that cost?
- How often would you do it, if you didn't have to worry about working fixed hours?
- If money were no longer an issue, what would you do for fun?

_____

Have you ever been in a home business before?

[If YES]:

- When?

HERE ARE YOUR INTERVIEW QUESTIONS

- Which one(s)?
- What happened?
- What did you like/dislike about it?

[If NO]:

- Why not?

_____

How important is it to you to work with someone who is experienced?

_____

Are you someone who is willing to follow directions, or are you more the type to do things your own way?

- Did you go through training for your current job?
- Have you ever been on a sports team, or had a coach?
- Would you consider yourself coachable?

_____

Do you mostly use a computer, a tablet, or your phone?

_____

Are you on any social media, like Facebook or LinkedIn?

_____

Is there anyone else involved in the decision-making process to start a home business? Will you be asking someone else for approval?

- Who?
- Why?

- We should involve them in this conversation then, shouldn't we?

_____

What would you say are some of your BEST characteristics?

- How persistent are you?
- How good is your word?
- Would others consider you a reliable person?

_____

Tell me some reasons why someone would want to work with you and help you build a home business.

_____

If I give you materials to look at and review, are you the type of person who would go through them thoroughly, or probably not so much?

_____

HOW SOON could you review the information I'm going to send you?

_____

If I schedule a follow up appointment with you, *how dependable* should I expect you to be?

_____

BEFORE WE EXPLORE HOW TO CLOSE THE SALE

Remember, the more you use these questions in conversations with your prospects, the more natural it will become. But that can only happen through practice and repetition.

Always have these questions in front of you when speaking to a prospect, so you are never at a loss for what to say next.

By far, this will give you the greatest advantage when recruiting. Having the ability to skillfully ask the right questions at the right time is what will enable you to become a top-earning master recruiter!

CLOSING THE DEAL AFTER THEY'VE WATCHED A PRESENTATION

We've all been there — myself included. Picture this scenario: you've met with your prospect, shared your story, and presented your opportunity, and then the big question popped in your head:

How am I going to close and get the prospect to sign up?

It's a struggle everyone has had regardless of how long they've been in Network Marketing.

In a moment, you're going to see a series of 6 questions to ask once you are ready to close the deal. This is the exact same system that has been used by all the people who have become top earners and industry leaders.

However, before we get to that **6 Question System**, there are a few things to keep in mind.

Three points you must address to gain agreement from your prospect:

1. **Is it simple?**
   A confused mind says "NO". Keep your presentation, and your explanation of the business, *simple*. Don't attempt to 'teach' the pay plan, as that tends to be confusing. Cover only the highlights of your compensation plan in general

terms. The simpler your explanations are, the easier it is for your prospect to say "YES".

2. Does it Work?

Tell your personal story of how the product/service worked for you. Talk about how the business has helped you in your life. Show and talk about several real-life testimonials of people who are similar to your prospect. Always remember, "Facts tell. Stories SELL".

3. Can I Do it?

No matter how good your company, your products/service, or your presentation is... your prospects will say "NO" if they can't see themselves doing it. Help them visualize the benefits they have to gain. Have them imagine how this would solve their problems. Have them tell you how their lives would be improved by using your products/services and earning additional money. When THEY tell YOU, it allows them to visualize their own success.

THE 6 QUESTION SYSTEM TO CLOSING THE DEAL

I have a simple closing methodology that works with every company and works in every country. This is time-tested and proven to work with every age group and gender. Best of all, it consists of only 6 QUESTIONS.

#1. What did you like best?

At the end of every exposure, the most effective question you can start with is ***"What did you like best?"***

The worst question you could ask is "*What did you think?*" Asking what your prospect thinks invites the critic. They begin to think of how they could critique your presentation, and they come up with negative thoughts.

When you ask ***"What did you like best?"***, you'll get completely different answers. This question invites positive thoughts. In fact, their answers will give you clues as to their level of interest. If they really liked the product, that'll guide you in a particular direction as you go forward. Or if they like the residual income, flexibility, or the people, then you'll know to focus on those things.

#2. On a Scale of 1 to 10...?

Ask your prospects, ***"On a scale of 1 to 10, with 1 being 'Not at*** *all' and 10 being 'Ready to go', how interested are you right now in this opportunity?"*

This question takes their temperature. It will help you gauge their level of interest and how much more help they might need to make a decision. You will get a lot of 6's, 7s', and 8's. And that's great! You can follow up with *"Why did you give yourself that number?"* to gain more information and let them hear themselves talk about what they liked.

But what if someone says 2? That's still not bad! You will have a lot of work to build them up to a higher number, but a 2 still indicates that they have some level of interest.

They might just need more than one exposure to get them ready. Just ask them, *"What can I do to help you get to a higher number?"* Their answer will help you identify what's the best follow-up to use in order to set up the next exposure.

Remember, anything over a 1 is good.

#3. How much money?

Now we start asking hypothetical questions. **"Based on what you've just seen, if you were to get started with this company on a part-time basis, approximately how much money would you need to earn per month in order to make this worth your time?"**

ASK what level of income would be interesting for them. Don't TELL them what they could make. Listen to find out what they want, what their dreams are.

Be aware that some people will hit you with completely unrealistic pie-in-the-sky numbers. If that happens, you can help ground them by asking (or reminding them) how much they make on their full-time job now and how long have they worked there.

THE 6 QUESTION SYSTEM TO CLOSING THE DEAL

#4. How many hours?

"Approximately how many hours could you commit each week to develop that kind of income?"

Again, listen to what they are willing to do, rather than making a suggestion.

Remember, in your initial conversation, you asked them this question earlier: *"Provided that you qualify, how much time would you be willing to invest in a business venture on a weekly basis?"*

Are they being consistent? If so, great. If not, listen for what may have changed. You may need to remind them of their initial response to that question.

#5. How many months?

How many months would you work (X) hours a week (use their previous answer) in order to develop that kind of income?

Find out how much time they're willing to invest to get to the level they want to reach.

Once again, some people are not going to be realistic with you. It's good to compare what they are earning on their current full-time job, and how long it took them to get there.

#6. If I... would you?

***"IF I** could show you how to develop an income of (their answer to #3) per month, working (their answer to #4) hours a week over the course of (their answer to #5) months, **WOULD YOU** be ready to get started now?"*

All you are doing is asking them what their dream is. Then, if you could give them their dream, would they take action on it?

Most people will respond positively. I mean, who wouldn't want to achieve their dreams?

ACT AS AN ADVISOR

As we discussed earlier, occasionally you'll get some crazy answers to some of these questions.

Suppose someone says they want to make $20,000 a month, working only 5 hours a week, and they'll give you 2 months to accomplish that.

You have to remember that you are acting as an ADVISOR for your prospects. And as such, you'll have to be realistic with them. It's OK to compare it to what they're doing now and then guide them back to more realistic thinking.

You'll have to tell them that one of those three numbers will have to be adjusted. It will either take more hours per week, or more months, or less money. But something will have to change.

Don't be afraid to do this. You will gain credibility if you are honest and realistic with your prospects.

CLOSING WITH CONFIDENCE

With this closing methodology, you will get more prospects to sign up because you are listening to what they want.

**Do not TELL your prospects what to expect.
ASK them.**

You may be pitching that they can earn $10,000 a month, when all they want is $1,000 to help put one kid through college or pay off a credit card debt.

The most successful people in Network Marketing LISTEN to what their prospects actually want, and then show them how those dreams can be fulfilled.

Use the **6 Question System** when closing, and your confidence and results will improve. Don't worry about memorizing those exact words, just learn the general concept. Follow this format and you'll be that much closer to becoming a TOP EARNER in Network Marketing!

LOCK-IN THEIR ANSWERS WITH THIS 2 STEP TECHNIQUE

If you want to avoid having your prospects change their minds about what they said, or 'backpedal', you need a way to lock-in their answers.

The 2 steps are to ask your prospects these two simple, but powerful questions: *"WHY?"* & *"ARE YOU SURE?"*

When your prospect gives you their opinion about something, or makes a statement about what they think, ask them, **"WHY?"** (or ***"WHY DID YOU SAY/SELECT THAT?"***).

Asking **"WHY"** gets them to reveal their rationale behind their answer. This gives them a chance to elaborate on their position.

Let me elaborate. You ask something like, "How much money are you looking to earn each month? They say $500 to $1000. You say, "That's great. Tell me why," Then let them run for a moment. Talking about why they said that amount helps cement it into their minds.

Sometimes, if they give you a short answer, or if the questions is really important, you want to follow up with a second question to really lock-in their answer.

You ask, "How many hours a week can you devote to your new business?" They say "8". You ask, "Why?" They elaborate a bit. You follow up and lock-in their answer by asking, "ARE YOU SURE?"

Asking **"ARE YOU SURE"** puts them in the position of defending and supporting the statements they just made to you.

Once they've told you why they are sure, they can't back down from their answers later. They have firmly committed themselves.

Use this 2-STEP COMMITMENT TECHNIQUE with any important questions during both the qualification and your closing process.

UNDERSTANDING REJECTION

Let's wrap up with something that EVERYONE has to deal with. Sometimes, your prospects will say "NO".

It doesn't matter how good you are, or how experienced you may be. It even happens to the most successful people in the business.

You will never have 100% success, no matter how skilled you are.

A comparison to consider is that even the very best hitters in Major League Baseball have batting averages in the 300's. That means that the 'best of the best' FAIL to get a hit about 7 times out of every 10 attempts.

It's HOW YOU DEAL WITH IT that matters.

Being 'REJECTED' doesn't mean you aren't good enough. It also doesn't mean you have a bad product or service.

It means the other person FAILED to appreciate what YOU HAVE TO OFFER.

There are 2 types of 'Rejection':

1. **"THANKS... but it's not for me. It doesn't fit my needs."**

   While this can be disappointing, you really can't take it personally. Anytime something like that happens, it's not a big deal. Sometimes, it's just not a good fit... plain and simple.

However, if it's happening too often, you need to go back and determine whether or not you're talking to the wrong people.

If you know that there are other people in your company who are calling leads and closing deals, then you can be pretty safe in assuming you are doing something wrong. Either you are talking to the wrong people, or you are saying the wrong things.

The good news is that by reviewing this guide and staying connected with the other training resources we offer, (like our live weekly training calls), you can easily correct whatever problems you may be having and get yourself back on the right track.

2. ***The direct "NO!"***

    This one will commonly happen when you propose your solution BEFORE you identify the other person's needs or wants.

    If you haven't clearly identified a problem they want to fix, then you will get a direct "NO".

    It is important to realize that <u>YOU</u> ARE CAUSING YOUR OWN REJECTION. That is because you are not being of service to other people... FIRST!

    After asking the 4 questions in your Initial Call Script, it's OK if you discover that the person you're speaking with is not a good fit.

    That is not the same thing as rejection. It is just a CONDITION.

    Simply go on to your next call.

CONDITIONS VS. OBJECTIONS

Frequently, people confuse CONDITIONS with OBJECTIONS. When someone says "I can't afford it", is that an objection?

The answer is… IT DEPENDS.

Let me illustrate it this way. Suppose you were selling yachts that cost *Ten Million Dollars*. You make a sales presentation to someone who comes into your boat showroom who is working a normal 9 to 5 job and earning about $50,000 a year.

When that person says they can't afford it, are they giving you a sales objection, or are they making a statement of fact?

Well, unless they are big lottery winners, or inherited a fortune, they are stating a material fact. They CAN'T afford it. No amount of salesmanship or skill can change that.

It is important to keep this in mind as you pre-qualify people, before you launch into your presentation.

It's NOT a 'rejection', or an 'objection' when you are dealing with a CONDITION.

Only through your skillful use of questions, and by paying close attention to their answers, can you know what you are really dealing with.

You may need to add that prospect to your list of people who don't qualify at this time. You will always be able to follow up with them in the future to see if their condition has changed.

DO NOT FOCUS ON MAKING A SALE

When attempting to decide if someone is a legitimate prospect for your business, products or service, your focus should NOT be on making a sale. Instead, you should pay close attention to identifying their problems and determining whether or not you have a solution.

Your focus should always be on helping to solve a problem.

You may discover early on there's no match there. It's not a good fit. That's OK. It happens.

You saved valuable time and you maintained a good reputation because you were never perceived as being offensive or 'pushy'.

However, when you offer a believable solution to their problems, your prospects will be EAGER and HAPPY to get what you offer.

"Find their pain. Then, be their aspirin. "
~ Matt DiMaio

ACRES OF DIAMONDS

There is a wonderfully inspiring best-selling book called *Acres of Diamonds*. Maybe you've heard of it, or possibly even read it. If not, I strongly recommend it.

It was written by Russell Conwell, a minister who went on to become the founder of Temple University in Philadelphia and also started two hospitals, where nobody was ever turned away for lack of money.

In his book, he tells the story of a farmer who sells his farm to travel far and wide in search of diamonds. There's a surprising twist to the end, which I don't want to spoil here if you haven't read it. The point the book makes is that people often have untold riches within their grasp, but sometimes simply don't recognize them.

Acres of Diamonds echoes Conwell's core belief — that each of us is placed here on Earth for the primary purpose of helping others.

Well, I am here to say that YOU have your own acres of diamonds with your MLM business.

It is not only something that provides financial gains to you and your family; it is also a business that encourages you to grow your communication and leadership skills. Those are important traits indeed, and can have far-reaching benefits to everyone whose life you will touch.

Taking your current business seriously will also make you a blessing to others. You will help them with *their* financial burdens, help them achieve their goals, and assist them in improving their personal skills.

All of that is a truly worthy undertaking, and one not to be treated lightly.

Always remember that we here at **LEAD POWER** are personally committed to helping you achieve your goals, and to assist you in bettering the lives of those around you.

The fastest and most effective way to grow your business is to have a never-ending, constant supply of fresh, interested leads for you to contact.

When it comes to the best way to build your business, there is quite simply NOTHING BETTER than a strong lead source. Nothing!

HOW TO ELIMINATE FAILURE

This is the ONLY way I know of that can enable you to completely ELIMINATE FAILURE. It is far simpler than you might think. This is not merely a philosophy, but a practical, actionable approach that is documented to work every time.

Here it is. Burn this into your brain. **THERE IS NO FAILURE...** *unless you quit.*

Rather than reading my humble attempts to motivate you, let us review and pay heed to those who have not merely spoken these words, but whose very lives stand as TESTIMONY to the proposition that YOU MUST PERSIST.

Read, re-read, then read again, and contemplate these famous quotes from the remarkable people who uttered them. Each of these luminaries came from completely different backgrounds and lived during several different ages, but all were in harmony with the simple but profound belief that you MUST NOT ever quit.

What these great achievers have to say was true then, and it is true now, and more importantly it is true... for YOU!

HOW TO ELIMINATE FAILURE

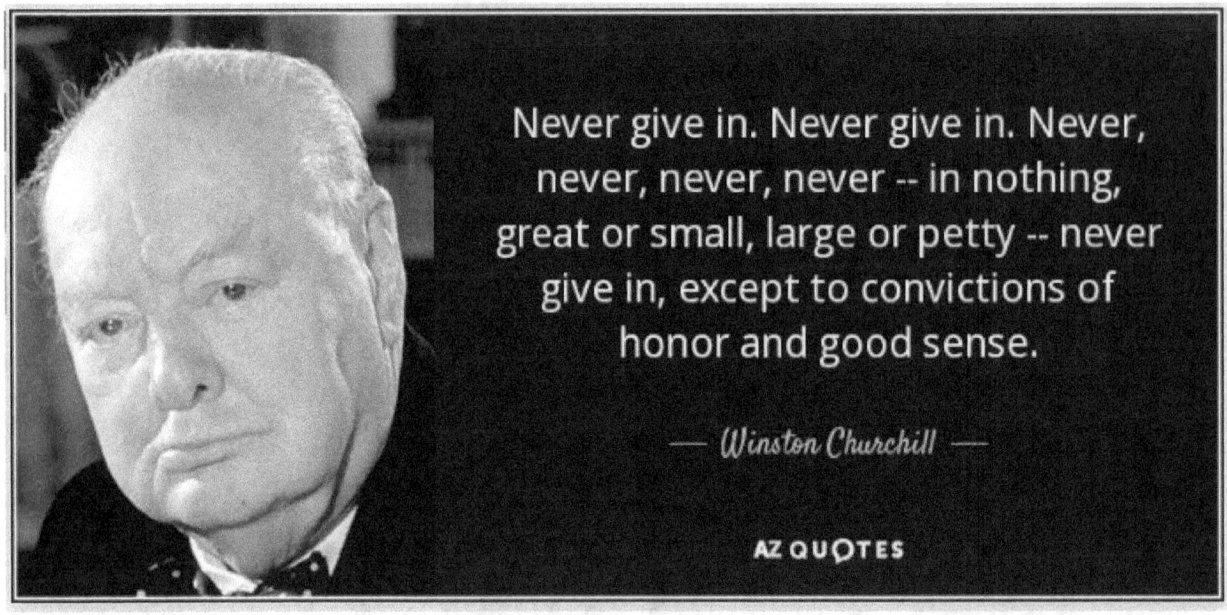

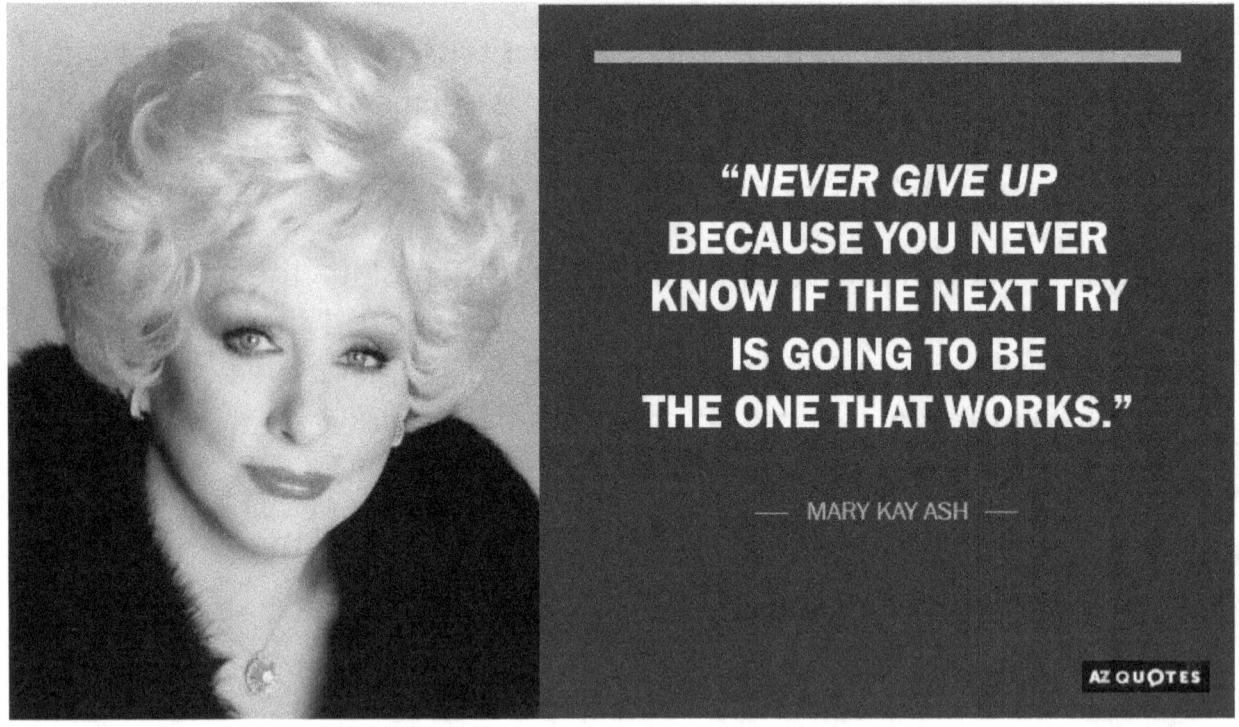

HOW TO ELIMINATE FAILURE

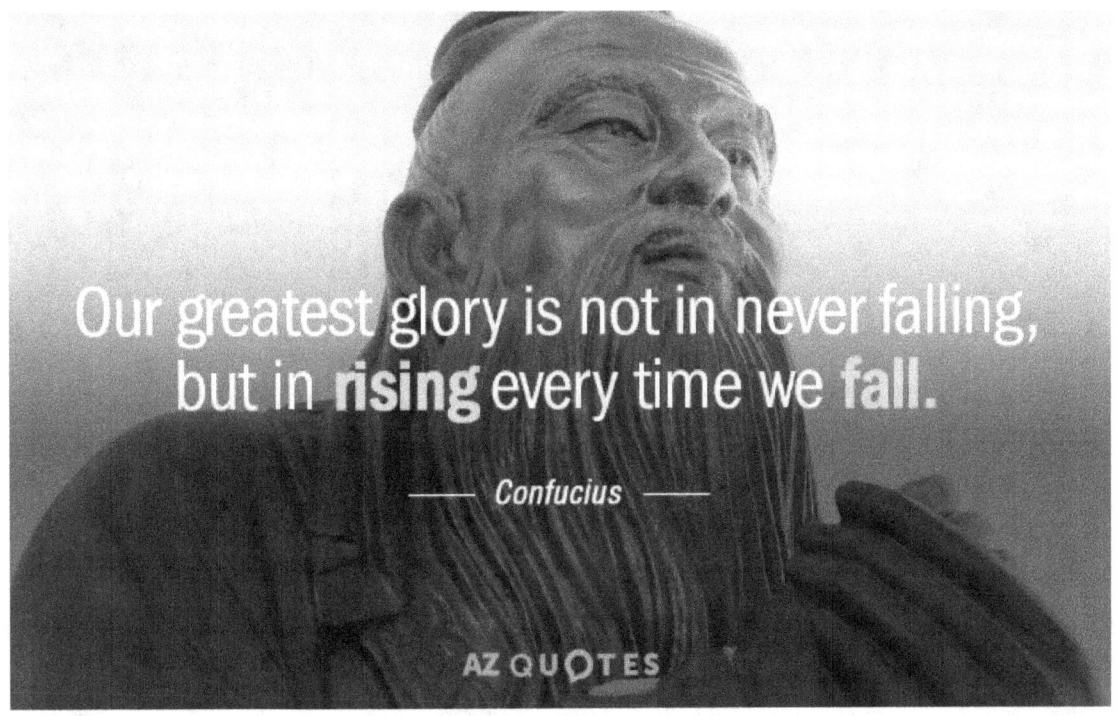

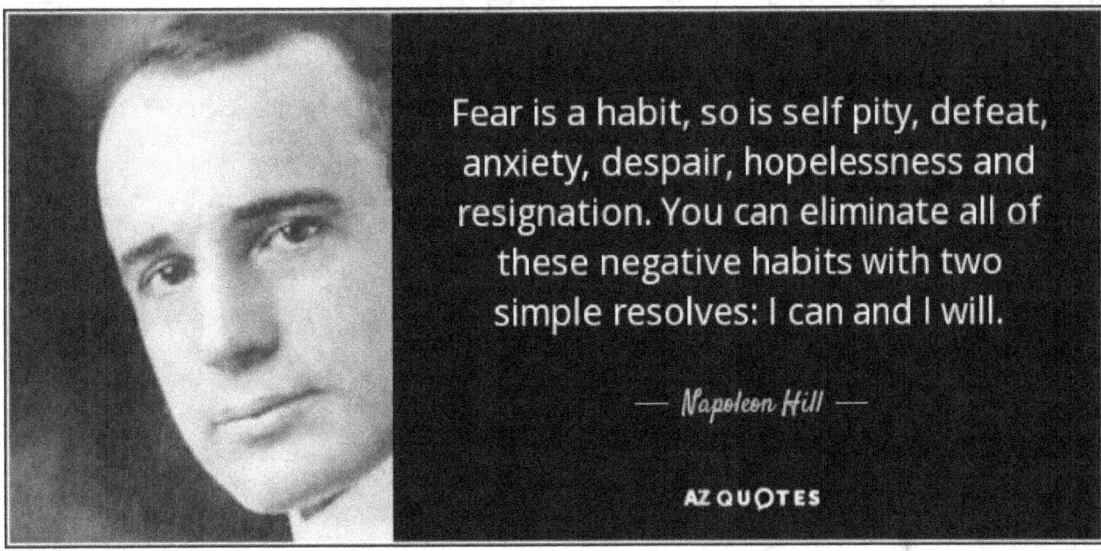

If you are serious about achieving the lifestyle of your dreams, you must overcome all the world's many obstacles and temptations that will take you off course and away from your true goals.

Stay true to your dreams, to your family, and to yourself.

We here at **Lead Power** stand ready to help you, train you, and support you in the pursuit and achievement of your dreams.

IN CONCLUSION

Remember, it is only in *taking action* that will generate the results you desire! Do not merely THINK. You must also DO!

The more you use the ideas, scripts, strategies, and techniques covered in this training guide, the more comfortable you will become with the entire process. That can only happen through repetition.

As you can plainly see, this training guide will give you a clear and obvious advantage when recruiting. Practicing and developing your skills with the techniques explained here can transform you into a *Master Recruiter*!

Network Marketing is about building a team. With the concepts and strategies covered in this document, you have been given a highly duplicatable process that can be followed by anybody willing to learn and grow.

Take the time to fully develop your personal persuasion skills. Soon, you too will be counted among those able to enjoy the lifestyle of your dreams!

I wish you all the success you deserve!

———————

RESOURCES

Free Live Training Calls 3X a Week

We provide you with ongoing free live training calls on a weekly basis.

In fact, we do them 3X each week: Tuesday, Thursday, & Sunday.

During these training sessions, our Head Instructor dials our own leads live, in real-time, and lets the audience listen to the responses from the prospects.

Then we do an analysis on each lead and what they said.

Doing this gives you a real-world understanding and provides you with clear insight.

To register for these calls, visit:
http://leadpower.net/livedials

Training Website

You are invited to register and get the first 4 training modules absolutely FREE.

www.MLMwealthtraining.com is a Network Marketing training site that provides 21 modules to teach you exactly what it takes to be successful in our profession.

Register here for your first 4 training modules on the house!
http://leadpower.net/MLMWealthTraining-Intro

Specially-Priced, Discounted Lead Package

Having enough people to talk to is *the key ingredient* to Network Marketing success!

RESOURCES

We have a very special package available.

You get 600 telephone interviewed leads for a truly amazing, discounted price.

These are all prospects we actually spoke with over the phone who have said they are interested in hearing about a business opportunity to work from home.

You get 30 leads a day for 20 days.

This gives you enough contacts to sort through and find the most interested and best qualified prospects for your business at a very affordable cost.

The price is only $135.
http://leadpower.net/135

We've got you covered!

We always provide an **additional 10%,** over and above the leads you ordered, to account for the possibility of any bad records.

Upline Coach Marketing System

The *Upline Coach Marketing System* is a highly advanced suite of automated web-based tools in an easy-to-use system. This fully integrated tool set is specifically designed for network marketers who want to recruit more people and build successful teams with less time and effort.

Far more than a mere contact management system, **Upline Coach** is an entirely new way to connect with prospects, make 'remote control' presentations that *perfectly follow-up* with everyone, and CLOSE MORE BUSINESS.

https://uplinecoach.leadpower.net

GOT QUESTIONS?

If you have any questions, you can call our office between 10 AM and 5 PM Monday through Friday. The telephone number is 423-536-6302.

RON MALEZIS

Author, trainer, and all-around network marketing authority, Ron Malezis is a pioneer in digital marketing. Ron founded LeadPower.net, the largest network marketing lead generation company in the industry, in 1999. Today, Lead Power generates over 5,000 leads weekly and has helped more than 180,000 clients find prospects, grow their teams and generate the best value for their business.

One of the top network marketers since 1980, Ron has built extensive teams, including three of over 100,000 distributors. He has a ceaseless passion for the industry and for taking new marketers under his wing to ensure they have all the tools and skills to make their own business a success.

Ron has a knack for distilling decades of network marketing wisdom into potent, easily digestible works, essential for anyone new to the field. To date, his eBooks and training guides have exceeded 200,000 downloads. Ron teaches marketers to present their businesses in ways that show their unique value and help prospects envision themselves as successful distributors and leaders in their own home-based business — because network marketers are not just selling a product; they're selling prospects on a business and a lifestyle.

Ron has been married to his wife, Jan, for 25 years. When he isn't writing or expanding his network, you can find him spending time with his five children and spoiling his three grandkids.

www.ingramcontent.com/pod-product-compliance
Lightning Source LLC
Chambersburg PA
CBHW081451220526
45466CB00008B/2587